A Cleveland Original
50 Years Behind the Lens

By Burt Graeff

With Ron Kuntz

Publishing Information

Published by
Cleveland Landmarks Press, Inc.
13610 Shaker Boulevard, Suite 503
Cleveland, Ohio 44120-1592
(216) 658 4144

©2009, Cleveland Landmarks Press, Inc.
All Rights Reserved

ISBN: 978-0-936760-26-1

LIBRARY OF CONGRESS NUMBER: 2008938029

Designed by
John Yasenosky, III

Printed by
Bookmasters
Ashland, Ohio

Front cover photograph of Ron Kuntz in his trademark Aussie hat.
(Ron Kuntz collection)

Rear cover photograph of Sandy Alomar, Jr., in August 1994,
which earned first place and Best of Show in Baseball
Hall of Fame photography contest. (Ron Kuntz photo)

Table of Contents

Acknowledgments

As my career is coming to an end and as I look back at what I have accomplished and the places the camera has taken me and the people who I met along the way, I realized how truly I have been blessed. So I first must thank my Lord and Savior Jesus Christ.

More than anything else, it was not the awards and accolades I have received but the many people I have met on my journey. For the awards pass away, but the ones who helped me I will always remember and cherish: my loving mother, who first introduced me to picture taking; Brooklyn High School track star Carl Weigand, who took me under his wing and instilled confidence in myself; my uncle Andy, who saw that my passion for photography was not a passing fad; and Eddie Dork, who worked on the photo staff of the now defunct Cleveland *News* and took me on assignments and showed me the ropes.

My family sacrificed much, and perhaps at times they felt photography was more important to me than it should have been. I have been most proud of my children: Ronnie, the oldest, served his country during the Iranian hostage situation and is still in the Army reserve; John, our second son, has followed my career path, now working as a staff photographer at the state's largest newspaper, the Cleveland *Plain Dealer*; Stephen, our third son, works at a marina in Vermilion, Ohio and is a jack-of-all trades; Rebeccah, (or "Princess" when she was growing up) who once wanted me to put her in my suitcase as I packed for an out-of-town assignment and who now lives with her husband and two daughters in Indianapolis; and Joshua, our Down Syndrome son who was born while I was in Moscow for the 1980 summer games and who later competed in the Special Olympics as a weightlifter.

And last but certainly not least my wife Nancy deserves more praise than I could ever provide. How she has put up with someone like me for 50 years is a miracle. I thank her for holding it all together – our family, our lives, and our perspectives – while I was away so much for work. Thank you.

Ron Kuntz
October 2008

Dedication

To my four aces – Riley, Julia, Caroline and Maggie.
Every grandfather should be so lucky.

Burt R. Graeff
October 2008

Greater Cleveland football products collide in a playoff game in Pittsburgh's Three Rivers Stadium between the Pittsburgh Steelers and Miami Dolphins, when Jack Lambert (left) a Mantua, Ohio, native and Kent State University graduate sticks Larry Csonka, a Stow, Ohio, native and Syracuse University graduate.

CHAPTER 1:
Ron Kuntz

Kuntz's first prison weekend at the Ohio State Reformatory in Mansfield, Ohio in 1973 shows Bill Glass addressing the 1,700 inmates.

Clevelander Ron Kuntz has spent most of his life viewing the world through the lens of a camera. And, what a view it has been. The camera has taken Kuntz, 74, to every continent.

It has taken him from the North to the South poles; to ten Olympic Games (eight summer, two winter), to the Kentucky Derby 38 times; to Zaire, Africa, for the Muhammad Ali-George Foreman heavyweight championship fight; to a coal-mining disaster in Kentucky; and to a flood in West Virginia, where the smell of rotting flesh was something he'll live with forever.

Armed with a camera, he covered one of the most famous trials of the 20th century - the Sam Sheppard murder case, watched in horror as

Cleveland Indians young pitching phenom Herb Score was struck in the eye with a ball hit off the bat of New York Yankees third baseman Gil McDougald, and visited nearly 2,000 prisons across the country as part of the Bill Glass Ministries.

Kuntz befriended Glass, a former All-Pro football player with the Cleveland Browns in the 1960s. "While playing football, Bill studied for the ministry," Kuntz recalls. "After he retired from football, I lost track of him, but I got a call from him one day in 1973. He asked if I would be interested in going to prison. "I told him, 'not particularly, but what did you have in mind?'"

Kuntz has been involved in prison ministry for more than 35 years. He has visited prisons

Former Detroit *News* sports writer and longtime friend of Bill Glass, Watson Spoelstra joined Kuntz during his first prison ministry weekend.

throughout the United States, as well as in Peru, South Africa, Brazil, Mexico, and Puerto Rico.

"At first, getting involved in prisons was not one of the top ten things on my list," Kuntz remembers. "In fact, I could not have cared less about those who were locked up. My feeling, like the feelings of many others, was that they broke the law. Lock them up and throw away the key."

Kuntz's attitude changed quickly. "My feelings changed on my first visit to a prison - the Ohio State Reformatory in Mansfield, Ohio," he said. "I remember standing in the yard with Detroit *News* sportswriter Watson Spoelstra. A couple of inmates approached us and asked if this was the first time we were ever in a prison. We told them it was.

"'We thought so. You didn't look too cool here,' one of them said. That's when I started to wonder what I was doing there."

Visiting more than 2,000 prisons has been eye-opening for Kuntz. "Now I see the inmates in a different light. I feel they need to hear the gospel and how the Lord is in the forgiving business. After all, we are all in a death row cell, waiting for our execution, because of original sin. But I believe Christ has provided salvation by taking our place on the cross, and with his shed blood, all our sins are forgiven."

One particular incident at Mansfield changed Kuntz's attitude towards prisoners and prison ministries. "A man from the Toledo area was

The last photo Kuntz took of Karla Faye Tucker before she was executed.

During his prison ministry, Kuntz also met Susan Atkins, a Manson Family member convicted of murder. He is with her at California Women's Prison when the Christian Motorcycle Association visited her prison.

attending a dinner at the prison on Friday night," Kuntz recalls. "He had been asked by a family from northwest Ohio to look up their son, who was in prison, and see how he was doing.

"Well, there were about 1,700 inmates there and the guy had no idea how he would find this family's son. He brought out a piece of paper with a name on it and showed it to the inmate seated next to him.

"'Where can I find this particular inmate?' he asked the prisoner. The prisoner looked at him. 'That's me,' he said."

Kuntz was struck by this story. "When I heard about that incident, I was convinced the prison ministry is something I should stay involved in," he said.

Developing a relationship with prisoners has at times been gut-wrenching, none more so than the relationship Kuntz developed with convicted killer Karla Faye Tucker. Tucker was a prostitute strung out on drugs in 1983 when she, along with an accomplice, used a pickaxe to kill two people. Kuntz first met Tucker in 1986 and took the last photographs of her before she was executed by lethal injection at the Walls Unit in Huntsville, Texas, 12 years later. She had spent 141/2 years on death row.

Tucker, a born-again Christian, was the second woman executed in the United States after the death penalty was resumed in 1976 and the first woman executed in Texas since Civil War days. "I

Kuntz's first camera was a Speed Graphic which he purchased second-hand in 1952.

Cleveland News photographer Joe Gazdak stuffed Kuntz into a trash can during a light moment early in Kuntz's career.

Kuntz in his early years with the Brooklyn High School Camera Clicks club.

knew there had been a change in her life when I visited her," Kuntz said. "She was a special girl."

Another well-known prisoner Kuntz struck up a relationship with was Susan Atkins, who was 21 years old in October 1969 when she was imprisoned for her role in a series of brutal murders committed by Charles Manson's self-proclaimed family during the summer of 1969. No woman has served more prison time in California than Atkins.

"I first met Atkins at the California Institution for Women outside Corona, California, in the mid-1980s," Kuntz said. "The speaker that day was Bunny Martin, at the time the yo-yo champion of the world. Susan and I talked briefly. She was warm, open."

Like many people incarcerated for a lengthy period, Atkins turned to religion. She became a born-again Christian in 1974. She married attorney James Whitehouse in 1987. She was no longer the same person who held down eight-months pregnant actress Sharon Tate while Tex Watson repeatedly stabbed her in August 1969. Atkins admitted saying to Tate, who was begging for the life of her child while being stabbed, "Woman, I have no mercy for you."

Kuntz and Atkins met again in February 2004. "She was 55," Kuntz said, "and had been in prison for nearly 35 years. Her hair was gray, and I did not immediately recognize her, but she recognized me, and when we met, I hugged her. A chaplain

Kuntz (middle front row) is pictured with the United
Press staff in Cleveland when he started in 1953.

Cleveland News photographer Eddie Dork
broke Kuntz in as a photographer.

"A Boy with his Dog" at a Cleveland Convention Center dog show
— Kuntz's first picture transmitted for United Press.

jumped in, saying, 'You do not hug the prisoners.'"

Kuntz and Atkins talked for about 30 minutes. "She said her spiritual life was the way she wanted it to be," Kuntz said. "I never was in any fear being around her because she was not the same person who had committed all of those crimes. She had become radically changed."

At the time of the visit, about 30 members of the Christian Motorcycle Association were present. "Susan hopped on one of the bikes, and we posed for a picture," Kuntz said. "I corresponded with her by letter in subsequent years."

At a 17th hearing in June 2006, Atkins was again denied parole. The next hearing is scheduled for 2009. Atkins turned 60 in May 2008.

As significant a part in his life as prison ministry has been, that was a commitment that came about over time. Kuntz's first calling was to photography.

Kuntz said it was his mother, Matilda Fellner, who sparked his interest in photography. "Growing up," he said, "I was interested in photography, archeology, and astronomy. I started using her camera and could not wait to get the photos back from the store."

There was no father figure to guide Kuntz. "I never knew my father," he said. After divorcing in 1946, Matilda Fellner married John Kuntz. It was not a good marriage. "My stepfather was an alcoholic who was abusive to my mother," Kuntz remembers. "I kept a hunting knife under

Yankees pitcher Johnny Kuchs throws his glove at Kuntz while coming off the field after a rough inning.

In an era when photographers were allowed on the field, Kuntz stands near third base to capture the action.

my mattress, thinking that if he became violent towards my mother, I would use it."

Kuntz was a tenth grader when he bought his first camera, a 4x5 Speed Graphic. The Speed Graphic subsequently gave way to 2-1/4 reflex cameras and today to the digitals. "I paid $250 for that Speed Graphic," he said. "My stepfather was not happy about it. He thought it would be a passing fancy."

Some passing fancy. Kuntz went to work as a copy boy for the Cleveland *News* after graduating in 1952 from Brooklyn High School in suburban Cleveland. "I couldn't afford to go to college," he said. Kuntz was determined to make a career out of photography and spent most of his early days at

the Cleveland *News* in the darkroom, listening to the photographers' stories. "I'd be eating lunch in the darkroom, and they'd talk about the gruesome stories they had covered, hoping to make me sick to my stomach. I learned a great deal there."

Kuntz's first big break came in 1953, when he went to work for United Press (UP).

"I heard about the job opening and applied," Kuntz said. "I probably got the job because I was young and they could break me in the way they wanted. I had no previous training whatsoever." Kuntz was 18 years old when he began covering the Cleveland Indians for United Press. "On my first day covering the Indians," he said, "I walked from our office at West Third and Lakeside to Cleveland

It was an embarrassing moment for Ron Kuntz. Indian Joe Tipton has hit a home run and is rounding third base. But then Kuntz trips toward the infield and Tipton had to veer around him before heading home.

During spring training in Ft. Lauderdale, Ron Kuntz gives Yankee slugger Mickey Mantle some camera tips. Mantle later signed one of his shots for Kuntz.

Stadium. I had a bag full of camera equipment on my shoulder. Some wise guy hollered at me that he wanted an ice cream bar."

It did not take long for Kuntz, a gregarious fellow, to get to know many of the Indians. "Dale Mitchell always spit tobacco juice on my shoes," Kuntz said. Covering the Indians in the 1950s was considerably different from today. Back then Kuntz and the other photographers were allowed to shoot on the field. "Once," Kuntz said, "while shooting near third base, Joe Tipton hit a home run. He rounded third and was being congratulated when I shot a picture. As I got up, I fell forward towards the third base line. Tipton had to go around me."

Through the years of covering baseball, Kuntz

developed numerous relationships with players. Among them was Yankees slugger Mickey Mantle, generally regarded as big-league baseball's best switch-hitter, a 16-time All-Star and three-time MVP in 18 seasons.

Kuntz was at spring training in 1962, shooting the Yankees in Ft. Lauderdale, Florida, for United Press International (UPI) (United Press merged with International News Service in 1960). During one of the exhibition games, Mantle was sitting outside the dugout and noticed Kuntz photographing the action.

"We struck up a conversation, and he asked if he could look through my viewfinder," Kuntz said. "I obliged, and he shot several pictures. A

When Muhammad Ali met with Mobutu Sese Seko, president of Zaire, Kuntz was knocked to the ground by some foreign photographers and when Kuntz stood up he was in the inner circle and was able to get a clear shot.

Muhammad Ali playfully pummels Kuntz when they met at Churchill Downs.

photographer nearby, noting the byplay, took some pictures of Mick and me. I got him to sign one of the pictures. Mantle signed it, 'Best wishes, from one photographer to another.'"

Spending two months at spring training in 1962 turned out to be a defining moment in Kuntz's career. "When I first started with UPI," Kuntz said, "I was a bureau assistant. After returning from spring training in 1962, I was told that I went down as a rookie and came back as a professional."

Coming back as a professional triggered new assignments. Include among them: Muhammad Ali fights.

Kuntz shot several Ali fights, including the 1974 epic tussle with George Foreman in Zaire.

"Ali and I got to know each other," Kuntz said. "He showed up at a Kentucky Derby I was covering, recognized me, came over, and started playfully smacking me around."

There was a circus-like atmosphere when covering an Ali fight. Zaire was no different. A photo op was arranged one day at the palace of Joseph Mobutu, the president of Zaire. About 20 security guards flanked Ali and Mobutu. In the effort to get pictures of Ali and Mobutu, considerable pushing and shoving ensued among the photographers. "I was knocked down," Kuntz remembered. "When I got up, I found myself in the inner circle, and I had clear shots of Ali and Mobutu. The other photographers were yelling at me, and

Kuntz befriended many athletes, like Reds outfielder Bobby Tolan, with whom Kuntz played chess.

Indians shortstop and longtime friend Omar Vizquel organized a day to honor Kuntz at Jacobs Field in 2004.

Pictured and clowning around with AP photographer Julian Wilson at the American Golf Classic in Akron.

the guards finally escorted me out, but I got what I came for."

The relationship between the media and professional athletes was generally more cordial years ago than it is today. Kuntz, for instance, oftentimes played chess in the Cincinnati clubhouse with Reds outfielder Bobby Tolan.

Gold Glove winning shortstop Omar Vizquel is Kuntz's best friend in baseball. At Vizquel's suggestion, the Indians honored Kuntz in September 2004 by having him throw out the ceremonial first pitch at a late-season game. Vizquel was Kuntz's catcher. "I was as nervous as I've ever been," said Kuntz, smiling.

Not all of Kuntz's relationships with athletes

have been cordial. Yankees pitcher Johnny Kuchs was hit on the thigh by a line drive off the bat of Indians slugger Vic Wertz. "I was getting ready to shoot a picture of Kuchs coming off the field," Kuntz said. "He saw what I was doing, then threw his glove at me."

One of Kuntz's mentors in the business was Associated Press photographer Julian Wilson. "We covered a lot of golf tournaments together," Kuntz said. "He was a real character."

How so? "On the way to a tournament," Kuntz said, "I was following Julian's van when I noticed my windshield was getting wet. I knew the van did not have a radiator, so I could not figure out where the leak was."

14

Kuntz with Jane Fonda at a
Cleveland function.

Charo visited the Cleveland
Press building in the late 1970s.

Kuntz with Cheryl Tiegs
at Churchill Downs.

Kuntz with Bo Derek at Churchill Downs.

Jayne Kennedy caught up with Kuntz
while she was at an Indians game.

Kuntz found out once they arrived at the golf course. "Julian never liked to stop to use a restroom," Kuntz said. "He had a hole in the floorboard of the van and, using a funnel with a long tube, would relieve himself while driving. It was the first, and last, time I've been pissed on."

Wilson is one of the reasons Kuntz has been photographed with some of the world's most beautiful women. "Julian, noting that we were photographing so many famous people, wondered why we shouldn't be pictured with them."

Kuntz, happily married for more than 50 years to the former Nancy Knerem, has been photographed with Bo Derek, Cheryl Tiegs, Jane Fonda, Jayne Kennedy, and others. "I've never

really asked my wife what she thought about these pictures," Kuntz said. "She probably thought it's trick photography."

Others of note in the world of entertainment, politics, and sports Kuntz has been photographed with include: Bob Hope, Jay Leno, Drew Carey, Kevin Costner, Stephen Baldwin, Jonathan Winters, Tiny Tim, Jack Klugman, Willie Mays, Michael Jordan, Don King, Frank Robinson, Pete Rose, Reggie Jackson, Roosevelt Grier, Leon Spinks, Roger Staubach, Sparky Anderson, Don Drysdale, Bert Blyleven, Art Modell, George H.W. Bush, Henry Kissinger, George Voinovich, George Wallace, and Dennis Kucinich.

Kuntz was photographing the 1981 All-Star

In 1981, Vice President George H.W. Bush threw out the ceremonial first pitch at the All-Star game in Cleveland. He liked Ron's hat.

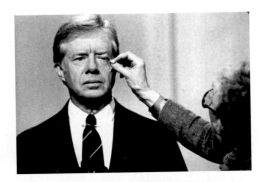

Best wishes to Ron— Jimmy Carter

In place of the not-too-flattering picture Ron Kuntz sent to President Jimmy Carter (top), Carter sent him back the signed formal portrait below.

Game in Cleveland where Bush, then the Vice President, threw out the ceremonial first pitch. Prior to the ceremonies, one of Bush's Secret Service agents approached Kuntz. "I had run-ins with the Secret Service in the past," Kuntz said, "so I didn't know what to expect. The agent said Bush wanted to talk to me. I couldn't imagine what he wanted."

Kuntz was wearing an Aussie hat he had picked up while on assignment at the 1976 Montreal Olympics. "The vice president wanted to know all about the hat, and how I got it," Kuntz said. "It led to a friendship. Every time we ran into each other after that, we struck up a conversation."

Kuntz has photographed every U.S. president from Dwight Eisenhower to George W. Bush. In

October 1980, he photographed Jimmy Carter, who was debating Ronald Reagan in Cleveland. "I shot a picture of Carter while a voice check was going on and he was being made-up," Kuntz said.

"It was not a very flattering picture. Anyway, I sent a copy of it to his home in Plains, Georgia, hoping to get it autographed."

Kuntz did get back an autographed picture of Carter. "It was formal portrait," Kuntz said. "I guess he didn't much care for the one I sent him."

Over the years, Kuntz learned that photographing sports can be hazardous to one's health. Kuntz has been hit by baseballs, and he has been run over by baseball, football, and basketball players.

Kuntz is reunited with big Frank Howard, former first baseman with the Washington Senators.

During the 1976 World Series, Red Sox catcher Carlton Fisk goes head first into the camera bay during a game with the Cincinnati Reds, hitting Kuntz head on. Fisk checks out Kuntz after the collision.

During a night game at Cleveland Stadium against the old Washington Senators, first baseman Frank Howard fielded a bunted ball and threw wildly to first base, where the second baseman was waiting for the ball.

"The ball bounced along the field line. My instinct told me the right fielder (Fred Valentine) would come over to get it. I turned around and Valentine ran right into me. My camera spun and a long lens hit me on the chin."

Down went Kuntz. Indians trainer Wally Bock came out, administered smelling salts, and escorted Kuntz off the field. Kuntz recovered in the dugout. Before heading back onto the field, Tribe outfielder Leon Wagner handed Kuntz a bat.

"Daddy Wags told me I should not go out there unprotected," Kuntz said.

Another incident occurred during the Boston Red Sox-Cincinnati Reds World Series in 1976. In Game 3 at Cincinnati, the Reds Ed Armbrister hit a pitch that bounced off home plate and up into the air. Red Sox catcher Carlton Fisk unsuccessfully attempted to field the ball to throw to second base for a force out. Fisk argued, to no avail, that Armbrister interfered on the play. A photo shot by a UPI photographer appeared to back Fisk's claim.

"The photo editor made an 11x14 print of the play and wanted me to go to the hotel where the Red Sox were staying to have Fisk pose with the picture," Kuntz said.

Pirate Doug Drabeck's bat flew into the photo bay in the 1990s. Ron Kuntz is on the ground.

Father and son, Ron and Plain Dealer photographer John Kuntz, man the third base photo bay in Jacobs Field.

The next year, the same thing happened – Doug Drabeck's bat flew into the photo bay – and photographers waved white hankies.

Kuntz approached Fisk, who did not cooperate. Later, at a restaurant where Fisk was having breakfast, he reluctantly agreed to pose with the picture.

That evening, in Game 4, Reds hitter Tony Perez lofted a foul ball towards the camera bay. Fisk, going full bore, dove into the photo pit - hitting Kuntz head-on. Dazed, Kuntz was helped up by other photographers. Fisk came over to see if everything was okay. "He saw me," Kuntz said, "hit me lightly on the side of the face, and said that was for all the trouble I gave him at the restaurant that morning."

Baseballs are not the only flying objects photographers shooting games have to watch for. Kuntz was covering a Cincinnati Reds-Pittsburgh Pirates playoff game in Pittsburgh. "Pirates pitcher Doug Drabeck was at bat," Kuntz said. "He swung at a pitch, missed, and his bat headed for the photographers' pit."

Kuntz dove onto the field and managed to avoid the flying missile. One year later, the same two teams were playing in a postseason game.

"*Sports Illustrated* photographer John Iaconna and I were sitting next to each other and commented on how we nearly were hit by Drabeck's flying bat the previous year.

Up came Drabeck. For the second straight year, he swung and missed a pitch. The bat came flying towards the photographers' pit. Kuntz and others ducked. "When things settled down," Kuntz

The 1954 Cleveland Indians with their families at Jimmy Dudley's home in Bay Village.

Along with actor David Birney, Kuntz was inducted into the Brooklyn High School Hall of Fame.

said, "several of us knelt and waived white hankies towards home plate."

Kuntz lost his job at UPI when the news organization folded in 1991. Since then, he has worked for Reuters, the London-based news and financial agency, while doing free-lance work for the Associated Press.

One of Kuntz's sons, John, is an award-winning photographer for the Cleveland Plain Dealer. "The funny thing about John's situation," Kuntz said, "is that when he graduated from high school in Elyria, Ohio, he had no interest in photography. He eventually went to Alaska, where he lived with one of my other sons, Ronnie. "John got interested in wildlife photography while there, and after

returning home, he enrolled at Ohio University, where he continued his interest in photography. I'm very proud of him."

Kuntz is overwhelmed when thinking about where cameras have taken him for more than half a century. "When I was young," he said, "I never really had the confidence to think I would amount to anything. I never dreamed I would visit the places I have gone to or meet the people I have met. Not many people can say they are doing something they love to do.

"I can."

During his long career, Ron Kuntz has met many celebrities:

George Voinovich

Jay Leno

Bob Hope

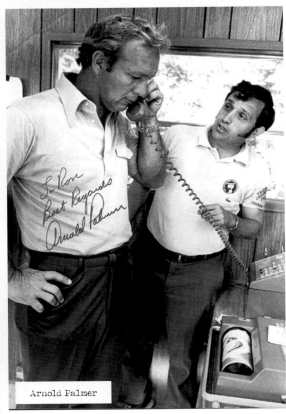

Arnold Palmer

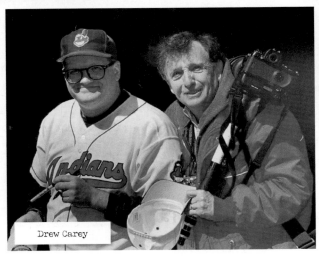

Drew Carey

Tiny Tim

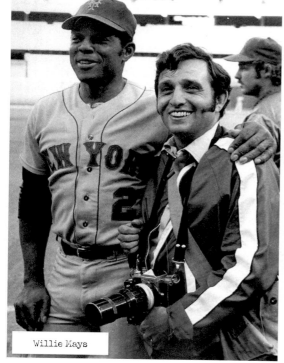

Willie Mays

Jonathan Winters

Jamie Farr, better known as "Klinger"

"Jesus Saves" Man

Pete Rose

Michael Jordan

Reggie Jackson

Sparky Anderson

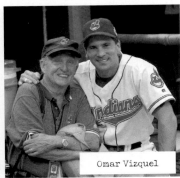

Omar Vizquel

Bert Blyleven

Roger Staubach

Otto Graham & Dante Lavelli

Don King

CHAPTER 2:
Baseball

Cleveland Indians pitcher Len Barker during a
game at old Cleveland Municipal Stadium.

There should be no fear involved in photographing a baseball game. Maybe so, but one of the worst promotions in the history of major league baseball ultimately led to Ron Kuntz fearing for his life.

The Cleveland Indians were averaging a paltry 8,000 fans at cavernous Municipal Stadium in 1974 when the front office came up with what it thought was an idea to swell attendance - for one game anyway.

The idea: 10-Cent Beer Night. Each paying customer over the legal drinking age would be given the opportunity to purchase an unlimited number of eight-ounce cups of beer for 10 cents. Oops.

The infamous 10-Cent Beer Night occurred on June 4, 1974, when the Indians faced the Texas Rangers. "Beer Night is perhaps the scariest sporting event I have ever covered," Kuntz reports.

It was not just the 10-cent beer that sparked what became one of the ugliest incidents in the history of Indians baseball. One week earlier, the two teams had engaged in a bench-clearing brawl during a game at Arlington, Texas. The 10-cent beer added fuel to the fire.

As the game in Cleveland progressed, more and more of the intoxicated fans became unruly. A male streaker ran across the outfield. Then a woman ran into the Tribe's on-deck circle and pulled her shirt up. Numerous fights broke out in the stands,

Texas manager Billy Martin holds a broken bat after he slammed it on the top of the dugout to ward off the fans.

Cleveland Indians Tom Hilgendorf is helped off the field after being hit in the head from an object thrown from the stands.

where there were 25,134 fans. The longer the game went on, the uglier the crowd got. It was clear that the security on hand could not handle the large number of fans running onto the field. The riot squad from the Cleveland Police Department was called during the late innings of the game.

"I was next to the Rangers dugout," Kuntz recalls, "when manager Billy Martin told his players to get the fans who had come onto the field. Indians pitcher Tom Hilgendorf was hit on the head by an object thrown onto the field. Indians manager Ken Aspromonte tried to restore order."

Fat chance. It was too late.

At one point, Martin used a broken bat, slamming it on the top of the dugout in an attempt to ward off fans. "Finally," Kuntz said, "Martin grabbed home plate umpire Nestor Chylak and told him he was taking the Rangers back to the clubhouse."

The game, which was tied at 5-5 when the teams left for the safety of their clubhouses, was ruled a forfeit in favor of the Rangers. "It was something I'll never forget," Kuntz said.

Besides the danger from drunken fans and the ever-present need to be alert for flying bats and players charging after foul balls, most of Kuntz's baseball memories have happier outcomes.

Ron, for instance, was present when Pete Rose broke Ty Cobb's all-time hit record.

Pete Rose liked to refer to himself as the Hit King. He officially became the Hit King

Cleveland Indians manager Ken Aspromonte looks bewildered trying to restore order.

Billy Martin tells umpire Nestor Chylak he is taking his players off the field.

on September 11, 1986, when he lined a 2-1 pitch thrown by San Diego's Eric Show into left centerfield at Riverfront Stadium in Cincinnati. The hit, the 4,192nd of Rose's illustrious career, broke Cobb's 57-year-old record.

Kuntz's picture of Rose swinging for the historic hit is on display at the Hall of Fame in Cooperstown, N.Y.

Rose, 44 at the time, had an outgoing personality, and it was never more on display than in the days and nights leading up to the record-breaker. As he approached the record, the media covering Rose swelled to more than 300 writers and photographers. The Reds arranged for Rose to hold press conferences before and after several games prior to the record hit. Rose relished bantering with the media. Seated at a table in a large room below Riverfront Stadium, he was thoroughly entertaining.

One night, a writer from the Washington *Post* stood up and asked, "Pete, where does all this drive and desire you put on display come from? Is it from your mom? Your dad? Just where does it come from?" With a straight face, Rose stood up, unbuttoned his jersey and said, "Right here!" Underneath the jersey, he was wearing a shirt with a large "S" on it. It was the Superman logo. The room broke out in laughter.

Rose was in a mild slump during the stretch leading up to the record hit. It prompted

Yankees shortstop Derek Jeter tags Indians
third baseman Travis Fryman at second base.

one writer to stand and ask, "Pete, do you think that perhaps you should pull yourself out of the lineup for a game or two?" Rose, looking somewhat incredulously at the writer, never hesitated with his response. "Ever see ceeeeeeeement burn?" he asked, referring to the sellout crowds at Riverfront Stadium that would not be thrilled at seeing him sit.

Rose grew up in Cincinnati, where he attended Western Hills High School. One writer wanted to know what kind of hitter he was in high school. "As a freshman," he said, "I hit something like .338. In my first sophomore year . . ."

Laughter drowned out the rest of Rose's response. Actually, it was his freshman year at Western Hills that he flunked. No matter. Rose had proven to be the ultimate entertainer - on and off the field. And Kuntz was there to capture the record-breaking moment.

There were also comic moments from the diamond that Kuntz was able to capture on film. Jose Canseco was generally regarded as one of big-league baseball's great sluggers, and for more than 15 years from the mid-1980s to 2000, he was a six-time All-Star, won the MVP award in 1988, hit 462 career home runs, and stole 200 bases. He earned more than $45 million during a 17-year career in which he played for seven teams - much of the time under suspicion of using steroids.

One thing he wasn't, however, was a stellar fielder.

One of the more memorable baseball bloopers, Rangers outfielder
Jose Canseco misses a fly ball, which then hits his head and bounces
over the fence for a home run at Cleveland Municipal Stadium.

The most embarrassing moment of Canseco's career (perhaps any major leaguer's career) occurred during a Texas Rangers-Cleveland Indians game at Cleveland's Municipal Stadium on May 26, 1993.

The Tribe's Carlos Martinez hit what looked to be a routine fly ball to right field, where Canseco was camped. Canseco went back near the warning track to snag it. He stuck out his glove. Amazingly, the ball bounced off Canseco's head and over the fence for as strange a home run as has ever been hit. "The picture I shot, which showed the ball bouncing off Canseco's noggin, was published world-wide," Kuntz said. Years later, Canseco was playing for the Boston Red Sox. "I thought it would be neat if I got him to sign a copy of the photo," Kuntz said.

Before a Red Sox-Indians game at Muncipal Stadium, Kuntz went to the visitors clubhouse, where Canseco was playing cards with several teammates.

Kuntz decided to leave Canseco alone, but some time later - before the Red Sox took batting practice - he approached the slugger in the dugout. "I asked him if he had time to sign a photo," Kuntz said. "He said he normally didn't sign photos and watched as I pulled out the one I wanted signed." Canseco looked at the photo, dropped back and said, "Especially not that one!"

Moments later, Canseco relented and signed the photo.

Baseball acrobats, Indians shortstop Omar Vizquel (top left), Twins outfielder Torii Hunter (bottom left), and Indians second baseman Angel Hermosa (right).

And there were certainly poignant times during Kuntz's career covering baseball, too.

Rocky Colavito was arguably the most popular player in the history of Cleveland Indians baseball. At 6-3 and 190 pounds, he had the dashing good looks women adored. Men loved the slugger for the long home runs he hit and for a right arm that was a weapon in right field.

Colavito broke out with the Indians in 1955 and didn't waste any time becoming a fan favorite. In 1959, he led the American League in home runs (42) and was second in RBIs (111). On June 10, 1959, he became the third player in the history of baseball to hit four home runs in a single game, blasting four in Baltimore's Memorial Stadium.

Colavito looked to have a long career in Cleveland, but in what became the franchise's most stunning trade, General Manager Frank Lane dealt him to the Detroit Tigers on April 17, 1960, for singles hitter Harvey Kuenn. Colavito's salary demands were cited as the principal reason Lane pulled the trigger on a trade that remains a hot topic of discussion more than four decades later. In 14 big-league seasons, Colavito played for six teams - including the Tribe twice.

Colavito's career was beginning to go downhill when the Indians reacquired him in 1965. He was traded by Lane once more in July 1967, a deal which Kuntz became a part of firsthand.

On the day Colavito was traded, Kuntz went

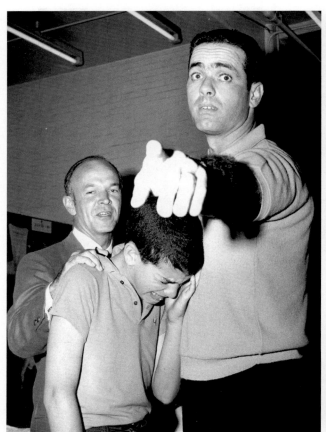

Beloved Indians' star Rocky Colavito shouts as his son cries upon learning that his dad was to be traded to the Chicago White Sox. Colavito threatened Kuntz that harm would come to him if the photo was ever used. It wasn't. Years later at Jacobs Field, Colavito and Kuntz reminisced about the photo.

into the Indians clubhouse, where a television reporter was interviewing Colavito. With his young son at his side, Colavito answered the reporter's questions. Asking Colavito's son what he thought of the trade, the young boy broke into tears. "Seeing this," Kuntz said, "I started clicking away."

The clicking stopped when Colavito, obviously unhappy that his young son was being photographed while crying, started yelling, "No, no, no." He charged that he would do physical harm if the photo was published anywhere. "I told him it would not be," Kuntz said. Kuntz did make a print, however, which he brought to the media dining room the next day and showed to Indians radio broadcaster Jimmy Dudley. Dudley subsequently

mentioned the photo on air while doing the game that day, and Colavito got wind of the print. "He was not happy," Kuntz said, "but the two of us never discussed it."

Kuntz was so unnerved by Colavito's warning that he shot the next two home games from the press box level.

Several years later, Colavito was hired by the Indians as a batting instructor. Eventually he and Kuntz crossed paths. "Whatever happened to that photo?" Colavito asked. Kuntz stammered. "I told him it was not published anywhere," Kuntz said. "No problem," Colavito replied. "How can I get a couple of prints?" Colavito asked.

"How many do you want?" replied Kuntz, relieved.

More memorable baseball moments: President Bill Clinton throws out the first pitch in the 1994 inaugural game at Jacobs Field (top right), Kansas City Royals pitchers seek recognition (bottom right), Yankees manager Casey Stengel fumes after the Yankees dropped the first game of a 1954 doubleheader (bottom left), and the Minnesota Twins keep their feet dry in a flooded dugout in Cleveland Municipal Stadium (top left).

31

CHAPTER 3:
Football

Ron Kuntz met with Art Modell many times when he was the owner of the Cleveland Browns.

Art Modell bashers, and there are plenty of them in Cleveland, will be happy to hear that the former Browns owner claimed Ron Kuntz once cost him $50,000.

Modell, who owned the Browns from 1961 until 1995, when he moved them to Baltimore, took over control of Cleveland Municipal Stadium in 1973. In doing so, he assumed all operating costs for the stadium, which housed the NFL's Browns and the American League's Indians.

After home plate was moved 15 feet closer to the backstop in the early 1980s, the lighting at Municipal Stadium became an issue for photographers covering baseball games there.

"Operations Manager Dan Zerby claimed that Cleveland had the best lighting of any stadium facility," Kuntz recalled. "I disagreed and asked that light readings be taken where home plate used to be, where the lighting was good." The new readings confirmed Kuntz's claim: readings taken where home plate used to be were adequate, but in the area where home plate had been moved to, the lighting dropped off dramatically.

Cleveland was to host the Major League All-Star game in 1981. "I had umpire Nestor Chylak put in a report to Modell that something should be done to correct the lighting," Kuntz said. "I also had the major newspapers in the area appeal to Modell to do something."

Something was done. One day, while setting up the darkroom at Municipal Stadium, Kuntz could

In one of the coldest sporting events Kuntz can recall shooting,
San Diego Chargers quarterback Dan Fouts calls a play during a
playoff game in frigid Cincinnati.

hear the sound of workers in the lights above him.

"Not long after," Kuntz said, "I was covering the Browns training camp at Lakeland Community College, and Modell approached me. He said he hoped I was satisfied, because it had cost him $50,000 to fix the lighting."

It turned out the old fixtures had to be replaced because they had rusted out and could not be adjusted.

Kuntz shot pictures of the Browns for more than four decades. Not only did he witness many great moments, he also developed friendships with several players.

Among those was defensive tackle Jerry Sherk, generally regarded as the best Browns defensive lineman of the 1970s. Cleveland's second-round pick in 1970, Sherk starred in football and wrestling at Oklahoma State. He played with the Browns for 12 seasons (1970-81) and was named to the Pro Bowl four straight years - 1973-76. Sherk, who ranks second on the Browns all-time sack list with 69, was named the NFL's Defensive Player of the Year in 1976. A near-fatal staph infection in 1979 essentially derailed what many thought might have otherwise been a Hall of Fame career.

"Jerry became interested in sports photography," Kuntz said. "I helped him set up a darkroom at his home in Medina."

Sherk spent one spring training with Kuntz in Tucson, Arizona, where they covered the Indians. He also accompanied Kuntz to several prison

Kuntz and former Cleveland Browns defensive lineman Jerry Sherk became friends because of Sherk's interest in photography. Here, they caught up with each other at a football game at Kent State University.

ministries. "Jerry is a real character," Kuntz said. "We were once at a prison in Huntsville, Texas, when he announced he had to get out of there. He said he could no longer stand being around all those Christians." Sherk took a $50 taxi cab ride to Houston, for his flight back home to San Diego.

Another memory Kuntz has of Sherk was when he was with several Browns players at a restaurant on Cleveland's west side. "The players, not wanting to be bothered with autograph seekers, were ushered to a back room for dinner," Kuntz laughingly recalled. "Jerry did not mind fans bothering him. So, he went up to the blackboard that listed the dinner specials, erased it, and wrote, 'The Browns are now available to sign autographs in the back room.'"

Another Browns player that Kuntz shot numerous pictures of was Jim Brown, generally regarded as the NFL's greatest running back of all time. Brown combined size (6-2, 232 pounds) and speed to break through the offensive line and demolish smaller defensive backs - amassing what was then a record 12,312 yards in just nine seasons (1957-65). He is still the only running back in NFL history to average more than 100 yards rushing per game. Brown retired at the peak of his football career to pursue one in motion pictures.

"The thing I will always remember about him is how he would be tackled by five or six guys," Kuntz said, "get up, and look like he would barely be able to make it back to the huddle. Then, moments later,

When it came to running the ball, Cleveland Browns running back Jim Brown was a force like no other.

he'd take the ball and run for 20 or 30 yards."

Kuntz became a regular at Brown's east side home during the holiday season. "I would go there to shoot pictures commemorating his latest 1,000-yard season," Kuntz said. "He was always very cordial."

After Brown retired in 1965, Kuntz ran into Brown when Muhammad Ali met George Foreman at the "Rumble in the Jungle" in Zaire, Africa, in 1974. "He was doing color commentary for television at the time," Kuntz said.

Covering football meant that Kuntz had to be prepared for winter conditions. Kuntz was on the sidelines shooting pictures at two of the NFL's coldest games played - January 4, 1981, when the Browns met the Oakland Raiders in an AFC

divisional game at Cleveland Stadium. The game-time temperature for the Browns-Raiders game was -4°; the wind chill during the game was -36°.

That Browns-Oakland game of January 1981 was won by the Raiders, 14-12. Of course, it was the infamous "Red Right 88" game, when Brian Sipe's pass late in the fourth quarter was intercepted by Oakland's Mike Davis. "Sherk was at that game, shooting for me," Kuntz said. "At one point, he yelled out to (Oakland's) Fred Biletnikoff, 'Hey, I'm Jerry Sherk. I used to play in the NFL.'"

Biletnikoff's reaction: "He looked at Sherk like he was crazy," Kuntz said.

He was also at Riverfront Stadium in Cincinnati on January 10, 1982, when the Bengals met the

35

In the January 1990 AFC Championship game in Denver, Browns receiver Brian Brennan hauls in a Bernie Kosar touchdown pass.

San Diego Chargers in the AFC title game

The game-time temperature for the Bengals-San Diego game was -9°; the wind chill during the game dropped to -59°.

The Bengals defeated San Diego, 27-7, in the game at Cincinnati. "Here's why I remember that game so well," Kuntz said. "At one point, when I had my camera up to my face, it stuck to my nose. The camera was metal. I had to tear skin off my nose in order to get the camera off it. There is no way you can get warm in that kind of weather. Your hands are frozen. Your feet are frozen."

"Believe it or not," Kuntz said, "these were not the coldest sporting events I covered. The coldest conditions I have ever faced shooting a sporting event was during the speed skating event at the 1980 Winter Olympics in Lake Placid, New York. The wind chill there was -40°."

Shooting cold weather events was hell for a photographer in the pre-digital days. "You tried not to shoot as much film as you normally did, because you did not want to take your gloves off to get the film out of the camera," Kuntz remembers. "Another thing was the static electricity created when using the camera's motor for multiple exposures. It would send an electric charge that exposed the film. The batteries in the camera went down much faster in cold weather."

"Plus, I always shot with my right hand exposed to the elements. I could never shoot with a glove on my right hand. Too bulky."

In a vain attempt to haul in a Jim Kelly pass, Buffalo Bills wide receiver Don Beebe lands on his head during a 1989 playoff game against the Browns.

CHAPTER 4:
Basketball

LeBron James is to Cavaliers fans what Michael Jordan was once to Chicago Bulls fans.

Michael Jordan was a 19-year-old freshman at the University of North Carolina in 1982. He was also a pretty good basketball player and made the winning shot for UNC against Georgetown to win the NCAA Championship game in March 1982.

Jordan was on his way to becoming a celebrity when several months later he visited three prisons in North Carolina. The prisoners loved him, and he seemed to enjoy mingling, playing one-on-one basketball with them. One of the prisons he visited was the Triangle Unit in Raleigh, North Carolina. He played one-on-one with some of the prisoners there, and afterward he talked into a microphone held by Bill Glass to answer questions.

Another visitor to the prison on that day was Mike Crain, a noted martial arts expert. Crain's specialty involved pulling someone from the audience and having him lie down on the back of a flat-bed truck. Then, Crain would place a watermelon on the subject's stomach, put on a blindfold, pull out a sword and cut the watermelon in half. Crain mentioned when explaining the trick to the prisoners that he had accidently cut 13 people while doing this. The prisoners howled.

Crain was looking for a volunteer from the audience. He spotted Jordan, who was sitting among the prisoners. Crain motioned for Jordan to come up. Jordan's immediate response: no

University of North Carolina freshman Michael Jordan joins Bill Glass for a question-and-answer session during a prison ministry in Raleigh, North Carolina.

way. But the prisoners would not let him say no. They egged him on until he finally relented. Jordan jumped on the back of the flat-bed truck, then lay down on a piano bench.

Crain took a watermelon, placed it on Jordan's stomach, reached for the sword and put the blindfold on. Ron Kuntz had the motor of his Nikon rolling when Crain pulled the sword back and came down with it to slice the watermelon in half. The prisoners went wild.

Jordan, dripping in watermelon juice, got up. He looked stunned. After things settled down, Jordan jumped into a car that included Kuntz. There was another prison to visit. "Not long after getting into the car," Kuntz said, "Jordan mentioned that he did not feel right." Jordan lifted his shirt. Blood was coming out of a small wound on his stomach. "We rushed him to an emergency room in Raleigh, where three stitches closed the cut," Kuntz said.

As he walked out of the hospital, Jordan looked at Kuntz and said, "I will never eat another watermelon again."

Years later, Jordan, playing for the Chicago Bulls, visited the Cleveland Cavaliers for a game at The Coliseum in Richfield, Ohio. Kuntz visited Jordan in the Bulls locker room before the game. "Want to go on another prison trip?" Kuntz asked.

Jordan smiled. "You still traveling with that crazy guy and the sword?" Jordan asked. Kuntz

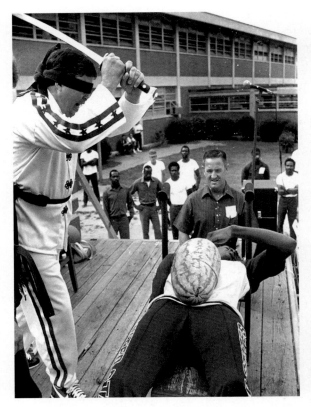

At the ministry weekend, Jordan was talked into having a watermelon cut in half by a blindfolded Mike Crain.

told Jordan that he was the last person Crain had cut. Jordan told Kuntz he had told several people through the years about the incident at the prison in North Carolina. "No one believed me," Jordan said.

The incident eventually proved profitable for Kuntz. "I once got a call from *ESPN the Magazine* wanting to know if I had a picture of Jordan scoring the game-winning basket over (Cleveland's) Craig Ehlo in May 1989. I told them that all my stuff was in New York, but I did have photos of a blindfolded guy cutting a watermelon sitting on Jordan's stomach."

The caller from *ESPN the Magazine* was speechless. "You've got to be kidding me," he said. The caller told Kuntz that the magazine would send him a check for $500 just to look at one of the pictures.

ESPN the Magazine eventually ran a blow-out story, which was teased on the cover. It read, "The day we almost lost Jordan." A sequence of the watermelon-cutting was used inside. Above the sequence, it read, "Michael's brush with death."

Kuntz also appeared on the *Inside Edition* television show. "I got couple of nice checks for all this," Kuntz said. "All this for pictures made in 1982 and shot, in of all places, a prison."

Of course, Jordan went on to become arguably the greatest player in the history of

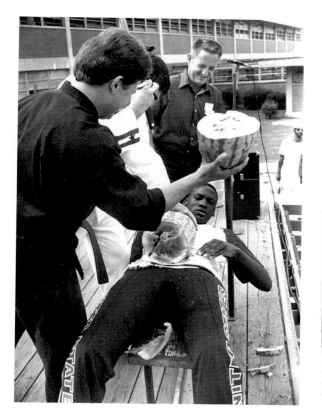

Jordan feels his side. He later discovers he was cut; after taking three stitches to close the wound, he leaves a hospital in Raleigh, North Carolina.

basketball. He was a dynamic scoring machine and a pit bull on defense while leading the Bulls to six NBA titles. No one terrorized the Cavaliers more than Jordan in the late 1980s and early 1990s.

"It is mind-blowing to think what could have happened to him on that day in 1982," Kuntz said.

The Cavaliers of the late 1980s and early 1990s were built around a team that included Brad Daugherty, Mark Price, Ron Harper, John (Hot Rod) Williams, and Larry Nance. This was a team, when healthy, that was capable of beating anyone in the NBA. "This will be the NBA's team of the 1990s," Earvin (Magic) Johnson said after the Lakers lost to the Cavaliers in a late 1980s game. The team of the 1990s never materialized.

The combination of severe injuries to Daugherty, Price, Williams, and Nance, parlayed with the most controversial trade in franchise history - Harper, two first-round draft picks, and a second-round pick to the Los Angeles Clippers for Reggie Williams and the rights to Danny Ferry - turned the Cavaliers into a very good, but not great, team.

Oh yes, don't forget Jordan. From 1987 to 1993, the Jordan-led Bulls eliminated the Cavaliers from the playoffs four times. The most painful to Cleveland fans occurred following

Lakers great Earvin "Magic" Johnson once referred to the Cavaliers as the NBA's team of the 1990s. The principals on that team were Brad Daugherty (top left), Craig Ehlo (top right), Larry Nance (bottom left), and on the opposite page, Ron Harper (left), and Mark Price (right).

the 1989-90 season. The Cavaliers of 1988-89 were arguably the strongest in franchise history. The team set a club record for regular-season victories, winning 57 games. It was 37-4 at home in the Richfield Coliseum, where the average winning margin was 15.1 points.

Years later, it prompted Daugherty to say, "There are a lot of things I will remember about that season. The thing I will remember the most, though, is coming onto the floor before so many of those games. Especially the home games. There was this feeling we had. You could sense it. It was a feeling that everyone we played knew we were going to kick their asses. It was an amazing feeling, one that I never had

before and one that I've never had since."

If there was a feeling of invincibility, particularly at home, Jordan ended it in a memorable playoff game played on May 7, 1989. The Cavaliers, who had swept the Bulls, 6-0, in the regular-season series, were deadlocked, 2-2, in a best-of-five first-round playoff series. They owned the home court, but it was Jordan's 17-foot double-pump jumper over Ehlo with the clock running down in Game 5 that kick-started the Bulls to their six titles. The 101-100 victory shocked 20,273 fans at the Richfield Coliseum.

"I have seen Michael Jordan do a lot of things," Daugherty said afterward. "I cannot believe he hit that shot, though. I saw people

running at him. I don't see how he stayed in the air that long and double-pumped like he did. I have seen him do some amazing things, but . . . they had to expect a miracle. They got it. His name is Michael Jordan."

While May 7, 1989, was one of the worst days in the history of the franchise, May 22, 2003, was one of the best. It was on that day that the Cavaliers, with 22.5 percent odds, won the NBA's lottery. With the stroke of luck came LeBron James, the 18-year old phenom from Akron's Saint Vincent-Saint Mary High School. The Cavaliers went from a team that drew a league-low 471,374 fans at Gund Arena in 2002-03, when they went 15-67, to drawing 749,790 the

following year, when they won 35 games. James single-handedly revived a franchise that went six years without a winning record and with no post-season appearances.

Now, for the big trick. Can the franchise keep James after the 2010 season, when he is eligible to become a free agent? A city holds its breath.

Kuntz photographed many of the NBA's giants, including 7-foot-1, 275-pound Wilt Chamberlain. Chamberlain played a memorable game at the Cleveland Arena. In the mid-to-late 1960s, the Cincinnati Royals played several games a season in Cleveland.

One of them occurred on January 25, 1969, when Chamberlain and the Los Angeles Lakers

LeBron James soars in high school at Akron St. Vincent-St. Mary (left) and with the Cleveland Cavaliers (right).

visited. On the morning of that game, Cleveland *Plain Dealer* columnist Hal Lebovitz wrote a piece, the thrust of which criticized Chamberlain for no longer being able to pile up the points as he once did.

Chamberlain, 32 and in his 12th NBA season, was averaging just over 20 points a game. Clearly, he was no longer the player who once averaged more than 50 points a game over a single season.

Maybe so, but on that night against the Royals, an obviously fired-up Chamberlain poured home 60 points in a 123-118 victory. Afterward, reporters surrounded Chamberlain and were poised to ask questions. He had one of his own.

Looking up from the chair on which he was seated, Chamberlain asked, "Where's the guy who said I couldn't score anymore?"

Lakers center Wilt Chamberlain scores two of his 60 points against the
Cincinnati Royals in a January 1969 game at the Cleveland Arena.

CHAPTER 5:
Other sports

President George H.W. Bush reacts after hitting his tee shot during a Pro-Am at Firestone Country Club in Akron, Ohio.

Lee Trevino got world-wide publicity for pulling a rubber snake out of his golf bag and playfully tossing it at Jack Nicklaus on the first tee of an 18-hole playoff at the Merion Golf Club outside Philadelphia during the 1971 U.S. Open. The antic, criticized by some in the media, was meant by the happy-go-lucky Trevino to break the tension. He went on to win the 18-hole playoff, shooting a 69 to Nicklaus's 71 in capturing his second Open.

The rubber snake, placed in Trevino's bag by his daughter prior to the Open, was actually introduced earlier in the week. Ron Kuntz was in the clubhouse on Tuesday night at Merion when Trevino pulled the snake out of his golf bag and tossed it at Doug Sanders. "I approached Trevino

and asked if we could do something with the snake out on the golf course," Kuntz said. "Trevino was all for it."

Merion's East Course was characterized by knee-high rough and pool-table-like greens. The United States Golf Association, which runs the U.S. Open, felt the rough had to be penal and the greens quick because the East Course, which hosted the event, measured a modest 6,544 yards. The course, which opened in 1911, sat on only 126 acres and was characterized by its red wicker baskets used to mark the holes rather than the traditional flags.

Trevino, who won 29 times each on the PGA and Champions tours in a storied career, suggested

Kuntz is in on the practical joke when Lee Trevino lifts a fake snake on his iron, scaring the gallery following him during a practice round at the 1971 U.S. Open in Merion, Pennsylvania.

he and Kuntz do something along the fourth fairway. "Trevino told me that one of the grounds-crew guys joked that the rough was so high along the fourth that they had lost a tractor in it." Trevino put the snake in Kuntz's camera bag that Tuesday night. "He said he would give me a sign to drop it in the rough along the fourth fairway the next day," Kuntz said.

Sure enough, during Wednesday's practice round Trevino gave Kuntz the sign while walking up the fourth fairway. "I dropped the snake in the rough," Kuntz said. "Minutes later, he came over and picked it out of the rough with one of his irons. It turned out to be a great photo, one that was run all over the world. No way would you be able to

pull something like that off with one of today's professional golfers."

Trevino was not the lone colorful character from the PGA Tour Kuntz photographed. Tony Lema, who won the 1964 British Open two weeks after defeating Arnold Palmer in a playoff to win the Cleveland Open at Highland Park Golf Course, died at the peak of his career in 1966.

Lema, 32, and his pregnant wife Betty, 30, along with their pilot and co-pilot, perished in a small plane crash on July 24, 1966. Lema was en route from Akron, Ohio, to Joliet, Illinois, where he was scheduled to play in an exhibition match after finishing tied for 34th in the PGA Championship at Akron's Firestone Country Club.

Tony Lema tosses his putter after winning the 1964 Cleveland Open, defeating Arnold Palmer in a playoff at Highland Park Golf Course.

With 18 major championships, Jack Nicklaus is regarded as the greatest golfer of all time. Here, he escapes the sand at Oakmont Country Club outside Pittsburgh, Pennsylvania, in the 1973 U.S. Open.

At the time of his death, Lema was regarded as one of the top players in the world - ranked just behind Nicklaus, Palmer, and Gary Player. Lema won 12 times and finished second 11 times on the PGA Tour. He defeated Nicklaus by five shots to win the British Open at St. Andrews in Scotland. Lema's engaging personality made him a fan favorite. He became a media favorite when, after the third round of the 1962 Orange County Open in Costa Mesa, California, he promised reporters covering the event that if he won his first tournament on the following day, he would treat them to champagne. He won, defeating Bob Rosburg in a three-hole playoff. The bubbly flowed. From then on, he was known as Champagne Tony Lema.

Kuntz photographed professional golf's Big Three - Nicklaus, Palmer, and Player - at numerous PGA Tour events for more than three decades beginning in the 1960s. How good was this Big Three? Nicklaus (73 tour victories, 18 majors), Palmer (62, 7) and Player (24, 9) combined to win 159 tour events, including 34 majors.

Shooting professional golfers can, at times, be touchy. Hearing the click of a camera can send a golfer into a rage. Kuntz discovered this while photographing the 1957 PGA Championship at Miami Valley Golf Club in Dayton, Ohio. "I had one of the scariest moments I've ever had shooting sports there," Kuntz said. Jay Hebert was on the 17th hole of the event, which at the time was match

With 14 major championships, Tiger Woods is closing in on Nicklaus' all-time mark. Here, he hits a shot at Firestone Country Club in Akron, Ohio.

play. He was dueling Walter Burkemo in a close contest. "I was using a Speed Graphlex that made considerable noise because it had a mirror in it," Kuntz said. "I took a shot as Hebert was chipping to the 17th. The shutter made considerable noise and scared him."

Hebert was not happy. "He came at me and started yelling," Kuntz said. "Eventually he calmed down, but I didn't know what he was going to do." Hebert lost the match, 2 to 1, on the 17th. Hebert's brother, Lionel, eventually won the event, defeating Burkemo, 3 to 1, in the 36-hole finals.

"Jay was there at the awards ceremony," Kuntz said. "He was still mad, glaring at me. The picture I took of him clearly showed that the ball was off his club when the picture was taken. I seriously wondered if I ever wanted to cover golf again."

---------- -------------- ----------

The Cleveland area has hosted two major heavyweight championship fights. The first occurred on July 3, 1931, when German-born Max Schmeling defeated Young Stribling on a technical knockout in the tenth round at Cleveland Municipal Stadium. The Stadium, completed two days earlier, was hosting its first sporting event. Tickets ranged from $3 to $25.

Kuntz photographed the second, and last, major heavyweight fight held in the Cleveland area. On March 24, 1975, Muhammad Ali met huge underdog Chuck Wepner at The Coliseum

Arnold Palmer, who won the 1954 U.S. Amateur Championship while stationed with the Coast Guard in Cleveland, has earned his title as the general of "Arnie's Army."

Gary Player reacts after making a putt in a playoff at Firestone Country Club in Akron, Ohio.

in Richfield. Ali was the reigning heavyweight champ, having knocked out George Foreman five months earlier in Zaire, an event Kuntz also covered. Wepner went into the fight, promoted by flamboyant Clevelander Don King, as a 30-1 underdog.

While Ali was already known as "The Greatest," Wepner, an ex-Marine from Bayonne, New Jersey, was known as the "Bayonne Bleeder." And, with good reason. It is estimated that over a career in which he won 31 fights, lost 14 and had two draws, Wepner needed 327 stitches to close various wounds of his face. After being knocked out by Sonny Liston in a fight that lasted 10 rounds, Wepner took 120 stitches! Ali, who was guaranteed

$1.5 million, was expected to dispatch Wepner, who had been guaranteed $100,000, with ease.

It didn't happen. Wepner, inspired at the chance of a lifetime, went toe-to-toe with the obviously uninspired Ali. It looked to be a monumental upset-in-the making when Wepner caught Ali with a right to the heart in the ninth round. Down went Ali, for an eight-count. There are some who insist Ali slipped.

Whatever the case, the knockdown woke Ali up. Angered, he went on to win on a TKO in the 15th round, breaking Wepner's nose and jaw along the way.

The fight was witnessed by more than 14,000 fans, who paid from $10 to $75 for tickets at the

50

The last time Cleveland hosted a major title bout was the 1975 Muhammad Ali - Chuck Wepner fight at the Coliseum in Richfield, Ohio.

Richfield Coliseum. Among those who watched it on closed circuit was Sylvester Stallone. Immediately after seeing the fight in Philadelphia, Stallone began writing the script for *Rocky*, which went on to win an Oscar for the best movie of 1976. *Rocky* launched a film series that would eventually gross more than $3 billion.

----------   -------------   ----------

Kuntz has covered 38 Kentucky Derbys, none more interesting than the one won by Strike the Gold in 1991. Joining Kuntz to cover the 117th Derby in Louisville, Kentucky, was Jack Murphy. Better known as "Murf the Surf," noted jewel thief, convicted murderer, concert violinist, tennis professional, and one-time national surfing champion.

Murphy became known world-wide in 1964, when he and two others pulled off the greatest jewel heist in United States history - stealing jewelry valued at more than $2 million from the American Museum of Natural History in New York City. Included among the jewels stolen: the Star of India, a 563.25-carat star sapphire.

"I first met Murphy at the Florida State Prison in the mid-1970s," Kuntz recalled. "He was serving a double-life sentence after being convicted of killing two secretaries in California." Murphy was released in 1986 and soon after joined the Bill Glass ministries. "I got to know Murf very well," Kuntz said, "and he accompanied me to the World Series, the Super Bowl, and three Kentucky Derbys.

Kuntz first met Jack Murphy in the early 1970s while Murphy was serving two life sentences in the Florida State Prison.

Murphy joined Kuntz at the finish line before the start of the 1991 Kentucky Derby at Churchill Downs.

At the 1991 Derby, one of Kuntz's cameras was equipped with a long telephoto lens. "I did not feel particularly comfortable using it at this particular race," Kuntz said, "so I asked Murf if he wanted to give it a try. I set it up so he would start shooting when the horses hit the 16th pole."

Kuntz lost track of Strike the Gold as the horses came down the stretch. "I had some great shots of the second, third, and fourth place finishers," Kuntz said. Murphy turned his film over to Kuntz to be developed. "Everything was out of focus, just as I figured it would be," Kuntz said. "But, then I got to the second-last frame, and there was a perfectly focused shot of Strike the Gold crossing the finish line."

Kuntz printed the picture and sent it to New York. The credit line read: Jack Murphy. "My boss wanted to know who this Jack Murphy guy was," Kuntz said. "I told him he was the only one who had a shot of the winning horse. My boss then wanted to know if he was one of the UPI photographers." Kuntz's response: "He is now."

Kuntz's friend Jack Murphy captures Strike the Gold winning the
1991 Kentucky Derby at Churchill Downs.

CHAPTER 6:
Award Winners

Indians shortstop Omar Vizquel arranged to have the photo pit at Jacobs Field named after Kuntz in 2006. (John Reid III photo)

Ron Kuntz has won dozens of awards for shooting pictures around the world for more than half a century. One award, for work during the 1972 Summer Olympics at Munich, West Germany, was bittersweet. "The Games lost a lot of meaning after the deaths of the 11 Israeli athletes," Kuntz said. What became known as the "Munich Massacre" evolved when eight Palestinian terrorists broke into the Olympic Village, took the 11 Israeli athletes hostage, and eventually killed them all following a long standoff. Among those killed was David Berger, a weightlifter born in Shaker Heights, Ohio. The Munich Olympics was Kuntz's first overseas assignment. At times during the Games, he could not believe he was there. "I was one of four

photographers to be on the infield at the track and field events," Kuntz said. "As I gazed at the Olympic torch in the background, I thought to myself, 'Here is a little guy from Cleveland, Ohio, covering this major assignment.'"

Kuntz also thought about Brooklyn High School classmate Carl Weigand, who had been a great source of encouragement. "For some reason, he took an interest in me, even though I was in the ninth grade and he was in the twelfth. I was small. I never thought I would amount to anything. Carl instilled confidence in me.

"He was killed in action during the Korean War. I mentioned Carl during my induction into the Brooklyn High School Hall of Fame," Kuntz said.

One of his most memorable assignments, Kuntz went to
the Olympics Summer Games in Munich in 1972.

Kuntz loved photographing track and field, and it was here that he took the shot which was named best of the 1972 Games. It was a picture of 16-year-old West German Ulrike Meyfarth going 6-feet, 31/2 inches to win the women's high jump. She became the youngest woman to win the event, then won it again as the oldest woman to win it in the 1984 Los Angeles Olympics. Meyfarth used the technique introduced by Dick Fosbury to win the high jump in the 1968 Mexico City Olympics.

"There were two other international Olympic photographic pool photographers shooting the event," Kuntz said. "Not wanting to duplicate what they were shooting, I went off to the side. Meyfarth did what became known as the Fosbury Flop, and because I was off to the side, I was able to capture her expression as she cleared the bar." In January 1973, Kuntz received a letter from the Paris sporting group informing him that his picture of Meyfarth was voted the best of the 1972 Games.

Kuntz's award-winners have come from various sports, including baseball, football, boxing, and golf. Here are some of them.

55

Kuntz's image of West German Ulrike Meyfarth winning the women's high jump at the 1972 Olympic Games in Munich, Germany, was judged as best photo of the games.

Muhammad Ali — Leon Spinks fight in
New Orleans, Louisiana, in 1978.

Kuntz's photo of Indians catcher Sandy Alomar, Jr., making
a spectacular catch of a foul ball off the bat of Detroit
Tigers Cecil Fielder in 1994 won first place in sports
action and best of show in the Baseball Hall of Fame.

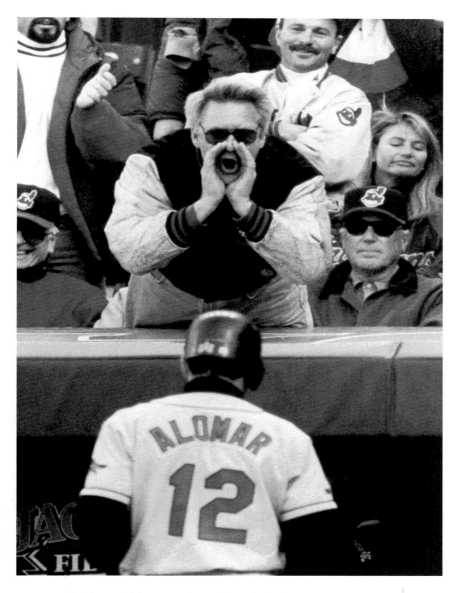

Baltimore Orioles star Roberto Alomar before he became a Cleveland
Indian, faced fans' anger during a playoff game with the Tribe. The
photo was taken a few weeks following Alomar's infamous spitting
incident with umpire John Hirschbeck.

Larry Holmes altered the face of Renaldo Snipes during
a championship fight in Pittsburgh in November, 1981.

Cleveland Indians first-round draft pick Jack Heideman is upended at
second base in the early 1970s. The shot took first place in sports action
in the Ohio News Photographers Association photo contest.

Ron Kuntz's specialty was the action shot. Here he catches
Indians second baseman Duane Kuiper's balancing act.

Sure-handed Reggie Rucker stretches for a catch during
Browns action at Cleveland Municipal Stadium.

Kuntz was in Cincinnati when the Atlanta Braves'
Hank Aaron tied Babe Ruth's home run record at 714
during a game against the Reds in 1974.

Despite a leaping try, Houston Astros outfielder Derek Bell finds the ball
glancing off his glove during interleague play at Jacobs Field.

Indians catcher Joel Skinner leaps for a high throw as Oakland
Athletics first baseman Mark McGwire slides into home plate.

U.S. speed skater Bonnie Blair rejoices in her win in
the 500m during the 1988 Olympics in Calgary.

A Cavaliers ball boy sprints to get out of the way of Atlanta Hawks guard
Jacque Vaughn, who had stolen the ball from the Cavaliers Bimbo Coles.

Rioters loot a dry cleaning establishment during the 1966
Hough Riots as a Cleveland police officer watches.

Air Force Thunderbird jets in a calypso pass
during an air show in Cleveland.

Indians outfielder Mel Hall looks for the parents of a
screaming baby handed to him.

During a tense 1967 hostage situation in Youngstown, Ohio, Kuntz was able to capture a mother tossing her child out of a second floor window into the arms of an FBI agent.

A demonstrator knocks down two Cleveland police officers
in the 1960s during a hard-hat union rally.

Carl Lewis anchors the U.S.A.'s 4x100 meter relay team that
sets the world record in the 1992 Barcelona Olympics.

Roberto Duran wins in a TKO over Lou Bizzarro in a
1976 lightweight title fight in Erie, Pennsylvania.

Cincinnati's Ken Griffey, Jr., connects on his 499th home run
during a game in Jacobs Field in 2006.

Sunset on the Ohio Turnpike in 1973.

Indians Paul Byrd pitches against the Seattle Mariners during a snow storm at Jacobs Field on Opening Day in 2007. The game was eventually called and rescheduled to be played in Milwaukee.

Kuntz caught it all, including brawls. Here, Jim Piersall
of the Indians takes a swing at Tigers pitcher Jim Bunning.

Secretariat wins the first leg of the Triple Crown in the
1973 Kentucky Derby at Churchill Downs.

Cincinnati Reds Pete Rose strokes the single that breaks Ty Cobb's career hits record.
The photo landed in the Baseball Hall of Fame.

CHAPTER 7:
People

Sam Sheppard (center) in a sheriff's car during his first murder trial in 1954.

One of the most publicized trials of the 20th century was the Sam Sheppard murder case. Sheppard, a Cleveland-area osteopath who lived in Bay Village, Ohio, was sentenced to life in prison for the murder of his pregnant wife, Marilyn, on July 3, 1954. Ron Kuntz was present for that trial, as well as the retrial in 1966, when after having served ten years in the Ohio Penitentiary, the court overturned the verdict. In the second trial he was found not guilty.

"At the first trial in fall 1954, I was there to primarily pick up film from the other photographers," Kuntz said. "I saw a lot, though. The atmosphere was circus-like. Cameras were going off during the trial. People were running all over. There was no order whatsoever. The media, particularly the Cleveland *Press*, crucified Sam. At one point, all the photographers who were shooting the trial were photographed in the jury box.

"This kind of thing would never happen today. The judge now determines if cameras are permitted in the courtroom. There were a lot of new regulations as a result of that trial, like the jurors being sequestered from the outside world during a trial."

The O.J. Simpson murder trial of 1995 was often likened to Sheppard's in terms of the media circus that evolved. In the Sheppard saga, Judge Francis Talty, assigned to preside over the second trial, made sure it would not be a carbon copy of

Photographers in the jury box await the Sheppard verdict in 1954.

Kuntz is pictured on the right as Sheppard is escorted to a courthouse elevator in 1954.

This photo of reporters getting credentials from the bailiff for the change of venue hearing prior to the 1966 trial earned Kuntz the ire of Judge Francis Talty.

the first. He ordered no cameras in the courtroom, no sketchers, no press table, no moving in the courtroom, and no statements to the media by attorneys or witnesses. "It was nothing like the first trial," Kuntz recalls. "Judge Talty made sure the atmosphere was calm."

Kuntz managed to get himself into some hot water with the judge. "Talty's bailiff was handing out change of venue credentials to the media, and I shot a picture that was moved on the UPI network," Kuntz said. Talty was furious. "He said he wanted to kill the photo," Kuntz said. "He said he also wanted the negative and the print. The New York picture desk was very upset, wanting to make a test case out of this because there were no principles

involved nor were there any courts in session while credentials were being handed out."

The judge threatened Kuntz with jail time if he did not receive the negative and print. The sticky situation was resolved after Kuntz and an attorney presented the judge with either a print or negative. "I don't remember which it was," Kuntz said, "but it was not both."

Sheppard lived four years after his release in 1966. "I got to know him and his wife (Ariane) very well," Kuntz said. Not long after Sheppard's release, Kuntz was assigned to photograph the couple.

"I was at their house, and Sam said he would have to ask her if it would be all right to get a shot of them," Kuntz said. She did not want her picture

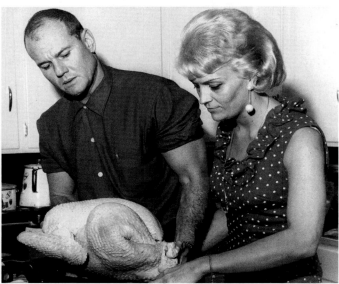

In 1966, Sam Sheppard and his wife Ariane had to deal with a second trial. Ron Kuntz was invited to their Rocky River, Ohio, apartment where he was able to take these pictures.

taken. "At that point, he took out a 9 mm pistol, removed the clip, and pulled the trigger. He said that someone had killed his first wife, and that it would not happen again."

At that point, Kuntz suggested getting a photo of him with his manuscripts, as Sheppard was in the process of writing a book. "He had the manuscripts in his hands and told me to get the pistol out of his pocket and place it on the mantle," Kuntz remembered.

"I had a silly thought - what if Ariane was dead and he wanted my fingerprints on the gun? I told him to give me the manuscripts and then he could place the gun on the mantle."

So, does Kuntz think Sam Sheppard killed his first wife? "I have talked to a lot of people about this," Kuntz said. "A lot of people think this was a crime of passion. There were 27 blows to Marilyn's head. I say Sam did it."

Over the years, Kuntz also photographed and befriended numerous politicians, among them Carl B. Stokes. Stokes became the first African American mayor of a major U.S. city when he narrowly defeated Seth Taft on November 7, 1967. "I got to know him well," Kuntz said. "He was very charismatic, great with the media. Everyone was caught up with the election that he won."

Kuntz said he occasionally worried for Stokes' safety. "There were people who resented him for what he had accomplished," Kuntz said. "He was an

Carl B. Stokes and his wife Shirley at a news conference in Cleveland after he won the race to become the first African American mayor of a major U.S. city.

Jay Rockefeller's 1967 swearing-in ceremonies to the West Virginia House of Delegates.

easy target." Stokes went on to serve three terms as Cleveland's mayor. He then became the first African American anchorman in New York City when he went to work for WNBC-TV in 1972. He died of cancer in April 1996.

One of the more interesting politicians Kuntz covered was Jennings Randolph, who served as West Virginia's U.S. senator from 1958-85. "I was sent down to cover one of his reelections," Kuntz said. "We flew together from Charleston to Logan, West Virginia. It was only a 30-minute flight, and along the way, he asked me all sorts of questions, like what I've done and where I've been."

There was a small group at the airport in Logan when the Jennings entourage arrived. "He

talked for a while," Kuntz said, "and then to my total surprise, called me up and asked me to tell the people there what I had told him on the plane - things I had done as a photographer and where I had been. I was shocked he did this."

Afterward, a writer from the local paper pulled Kuntz aside, asking how long he'd known Randolph. "About 30 minutes," Kuntz said, breaking out in laughter.

Randolph is not the only politician from West Virginia with whom Kuntz shared a light-hearted moment. In November 1967, Kuntz was assigned to photograph the swearing-in of Jay Rockefeller to the West Virginia House of Delegates. "I went to his mansion in Charleston to get some art before

England's Prince Charles in a 1977 tree-planting ceremony in Cleveland's Public Square. Later that day he lifted weights at the Cleveland Clinic sports facility.

the swearing-in," Kuntz recalled. "A maid let me in and told me to wait in the parlor." Kuntz waited for about 15 or 20 minutes. "Then," Kuntz said, "I heard some rustling in the hallway, turned around, and there was Rockefeller stark naked, covering himself up with the newspaper he was holding."

Rockefeller took the sting out what could have been a very awkward situation. "What a photo that would have made," he said.

Kuntz has even photographed royalty - Prince Charles, the heir to the British throne. "He came to Cleveland in the mid-1970s to take part in a tree-planting ceremony and to visit places he was interested in, like the Cleveland Clinic," Kuntz said. The tree-planting ceremony took place at Public Square in downtown Cleveland. "The Square was packed," Kuntz said. "I was near Prince Charles at the start, but got separated from him when he was to start the tree planting. Then, I was knocked down by an elderly woman and, when I looked up, Prince Charles was turning over the dirt. I was so close to him, my wide angle lens was barely usable."

Prince Charles later visited the sports center at the Cleveland Clinic. "I got a shot of him in the weight room," Kuntz said. "At one point, he came up to me and asked, because I was wearing my beret, if I represented the French press. I told him, no, that I worked for UPI." Later that evening, Prince Charles visited the Western Reserve Historical Society. "This time," Kuntz said, "he came up to me and asked if I

Kuntz followed Pope John Paul II when he traveled across Canada in 1984.

Cleveland Mayor Dennis Kucinich gets some tips from Kuntz before a Tribe game in old Cleveland Municipal Stadium.

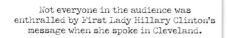

Not everyone in the audience was enthralled by First Lady Hillary Clinton's message when she spoke in Cleveland.

was selling onions. Apparently in Brittany, there are many people wearing berets and selling onions on the handlebars of the bicycles."

And the list could go on. From sports, to politics, to Hollywood, Kuntz has always kept his camera ready.

CHAPTER 8:
Regional Events

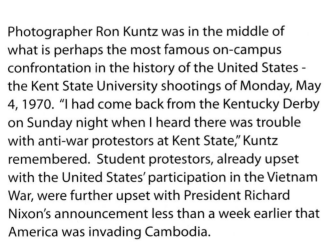

A Kent, Ohio, police officer removes a gun from Terry Norman, a participant in the Kent State University confrontation on May 4, 1970.

Photographer Ron Kuntz was in the middle of what is perhaps the most famous on-campus confrontation in the history of the United States - the Kent State University shootings of Monday, May 4, 1970. "I had come back from the Kentucky Derby on Sunday night when I heard there was trouble with anti-war protestors at Kent State," Kuntz remembered. Student protestors, already upset with the United States' participation in the Vietnam War, were further upset with President Richard Nixon's announcement less than a week earlier that America was invading Cambodia.

Governor James Rhodes sent nearly 1,000 soldiers from the Ohio National Guard to Kent to keep peace. The show of force did not work.

"I arrived at the campus around noon on Monday," Kuntz said. "The scene was tense. The crowd of protestors was getting bigger. The Guard ordered the crowd to disperse. The Guard then fired tear gas into the crowd.

"I took a picture of one of the protestors picking up a tear gas canister and throwing it back at the Guard." Kuntz followed the Guard, which marched up a hill between Taylor and Johnson halls. "I positioned myself near the entrance of Taylor Hall, but I was getting hit by stones thrown by students who were in the parking lot," Kuntz said. He went to the other side of a knoll for protection.

At 12:22 p.m., gunfire erupted. Over the next 13 seconds, 67 shots reportedly were fired into

During the May 4, 1970, Kent State University shooting, a protestor throws back a tear gas canister at the Ohio National Guard.

the crowd. "Along with the students, I hit the dirt," Kuntz said. "All the while, I thought the Guard was shooting blanks."

Of course, they were not blanks. When the firing ceased, four students were dead, nine others injured. For months after the shootings, Kuntz bemoaned the fact that he did not come up with a Pulitzer prize-winning photograph. "I was so close, but actually I ran in the opposite direction from where the shootings took place," he said.

There was a Pulitzer prize-winning photograph to come out of the tragedy. John Paul Filo's photograph of runaway Mary Ann Vecchio screaming as she bent over mortally wounded student Jeffrey Miller won journalism's most

coveted award.

Campuses were not the only places to experience tension. There was considerable racial tension throughout the country during the 1960s. The city of Cleveland was no exception, and Kuntz covered two of the most noted confrontations between angry African Americans and the police - the Hough riots of July 1966 and what became known as the Glenville Shootout of July 1968.

The Hough riots lasted over a six-night period from July 18-23, 1966. Four African Americans were killed, and 30 others were seriously injured as a result of the rioting. There were 275 arrests and more than 240 fires reported. Many believe the rioting was triggered when a bar at East 79th Street

Fire engulfs a building during the July 1966 Hough Riots.

The Ohio National Guard patrols a street
during the Hough Riots.

and Hough Avenue refused to serve an African American a glass of water. More than 50 people were gathered outside the bar when Cleveland police arrived. Eventually, 1,600 members of the Ohio National Guard were called in to defuse the situation which ultimately erupted into massive fires and looting of businesses.

The rioting had already begun when Kuntz arrived on the scene. "I arrived as evening approached on the first night," he stated. "It was dark. There were no street lights on, and I was ordered by the police to turn off the headlights in my car. I was afraid to use the flash on my camera, fearing that it might draw some fire from the rioters." Nonetheless, Kuntz was able to shoot hundreds of pictures.

"Of all the art that I made," he said, "there was one shot that was used worldwide. It was a picture of a store being looted as the cops looked on in the background. Later, I learned that the owner of the store said it was in ruins and didn't care what was going on."

The rioting was in full force when Kuntz encountered a surprise visitor to the scene - Indians pitcher Sam McDowell. "It was at 3 a.m. in the morning when a car pulled up next to me," Kuntz said. "Out stepped Sam. I asked him what in the world was he doing there. He said he was interested in photography.

"I told him that there must be other places a lot safer to shoot pictures."

The Ohio National Guard sets up a machine gun in front of a store during the Hough Riots.

During the Glenville Shootout in July 1968, Cleveland police and Ohio National Guardsmen are on the lookout for snipers.

The Glenville Shootout went from July 23-28, 1968. It began when a militant group led by Fred (Ahmed) Evans, a group suspected of purchasing illegal weapons, opened fire during a confrontation with the Cleveland police. Mayor Carl B. Stokes asked for the Ohio National Guard to aid the police. Four African Americans and three members of the Cleveland police were killed. "When I arrive on that scene," Kuntz said, "there was an overturned police car on fire, a battered TV truck, and a mob on one corner. I only took a few pictures, as I was suddenly surrounded by the mob, which was now angry."

Kuntz said that he was bailed out by Baxter Hill, a spokesman for the black community. "He said I had better get out right away or risk bodily harm," Kuntz said. "He took me to a store, the owner got his shotgun, and he escorted me to my car. A Molotov cocktail hit the windshield of my station wagon as I drove off."

On the following night, Kuntz rode in a National Guard jeep patrolling the area. Eventually, he jumped aboard a Channel 8 truck. "But," Kuntz said, "they had to return to the station and dropped me off at the Fourth District Police Station, where I monitored the story on their radio. Not long after, a shooting was reported.

"I hopped into a police cruiser," Kuntz said. "We arrived at the scene as someone fired a bullet into the rear view mirror of a jeep. To my amazement, it was the jeep I had been riding in earlier that night.

Players and their wives rush out onto the field when an earthquake measuring 6.9 on the Richter Scale, before Game 3 of the 1989 World Series, between the San Francisco Giants and the Oakland Athletics.

A 1965 Palm Sunday tornado in Lorain County, Ohio, wiped out the entire town of Pittsfield.

San Francisco Giants outfielder Brett Butler, his wife Eveline (right), and his mother-in-law react after an aftershock hit before Game 3.

Had I been in that jeep, I might have taken a bullet."

Kuntz also covered numerous calamities - floods, tornados, and fires. Nothing prepared him for what occurred moments before Game 3 of the 1989 World Series at Candlestick Park in San Francisco, California. The Oakland A's and San Francisco Giants were about ready to begin play on October 17, 1989, when an earthquake measuring 6.9 on the Richter scale and lasting 15 seconds hit Northern California. What became known as the Loma Prieta earthquake struck at 5:04 p.m. "It was the most helpless feeling I've ever experienced," said Kuntz, who was covering the series from the press box level, not on the field.

"It was my first time covering games from

the press box," he said. "At the time the quake hit, I thought it was kids banging on stadium seats. Then the stadium started to sway, and one of the photographers from California yelled out that we were having an earthquake.

"It was a frightening experience. I didn't know where to go, what to do. Players from both teams made their way onto the field. The aftershocks scared me as much as anything."

The Loma Prieta earthquake ultimately killed 67 people and injured nearly 4,000 others. Property damage was estimated at $6 billion. The series, eventually won in a four-game sweep by the A's, was delayed 10 days before the start of Game 3.

The quake proved to be a logistical nightmare

UPI staff photographers set up a makeshift work area to transmit pictures.

Damage from the 1989 earthquake near Candlestick Park was extensive.

for Kuntz, along with the other photographers. "All the power, as well as the phone service, went out," he said. "We were able to process film, but not dry it. We had to waive the film in the air. Eventually, we used the power and phone lines from the TV trucks to send out pictures. I felt very fortunate to have survived all of this."

CHAPTER 9: Travels

Near the ice caves at McMurdo Sound in Antarctica.

Ron Kuntz's travels have taken him from the top of the world to the bottom. Literally. He and his camera have spent time at both the North and South poles. "I can't imagine many people being able to say they've done that," he commented.

Kuntz was in the Army when the Pentagon assigned him to photograph the resupplying of the Distant Early Warning (DEW) Line sites above the Arctic Circle in July 1958. The DEW Line was a radar system set up in the Arctic regions of Canada to detect any attacks from over the North Pole. Kuntz spent two months aboard the USNS *Point Barrow* photographing the operation, the weather, and the terrain.

The *Point Barrow*, specially designed for Arctic operations, was a 456-foot, 10.3-ton ship. "The whole experience was something I will never forget," Kuntz said. "One night we ran into a storm in the Davis Straight. The ship took 27-degree rolls. I tried to take a shower that night, but could not get wet because the water was moving back and forth so much."

There were other unforgettable moments. "I was playing chess with a Navy guy one night when a sailor on watch hollered for us to come to the bow of the ship," Kuntz recalled. "We were treated to a spectacular sight - the aurora borealis [also known as the northern lights], wavy streams in the sky of reds, greens, and yellows."

When Kuntz was in Moscow for the 1980 Olympic Games, he took this interesting shot of Red Square from St. Basil's Cathedral.

Two months aboard the USNS *Point Barrow* was followed by two weeks at Thule Air Force Base in Thule, Greenland. While at Thule AFB, Kuntz visited Greenland's ice cap, the second largest ice mass in the world behind Antarctica. "As I looked at the great expanse of whiteness," Kuntz said, "I thought that I was glad I'd never have to see that place again."

Wrong. Several months later, he was assigned to a project called Camp Century. The location? Greenland's ice cap, 600 miles from the North Pole. Greenland's ice cap covers about 82 percent of the country. At its center, it is 10,000 feet thick. Kuntz spent four months on the ice cap.

"For three of those months," he said, "I never saw night. The sun just circled overhead. I remember 18 of us Army guys watching the sun disappear on August 23rd at about 2:30 in the morning and popping up above the horizon moments later."

Whiteouts on the ice cap were extremely dangerous. "It was the worst feared thing about being there," Kuntz declared. "It was a fog condition that cannot be determined, unlike when you can see a storm approaching." Kuntz learned first-hand about the dangers of whiteouts.

"I was walking away from the temporary camp one day along an experimental trench," he said. "I didn't hear the generator of the camp and suddenly found myself in complete whiteness. I could not even see the Army-issue black gloves on my hands. I knew I was in trouble. We were warned to never

This 1988 aerial view shows how Hong Kong has dealt with its space limitations: by building toward the sky.

Surviving in Havana, Cuba, requires ingenuity.

try to get back from where you started. You think you're going straight, but actually, you end up going in a circle. Exhaustion follows, you want to go to sleep, and you never wake up."

Kuntz managed to find his way to a trench. "I had my back against a wall of snow," he said. "There was no sound. My mind started playing tricks on me." Several weeks earlier, there had been reports of a polar bear and cub near the camp site. I did have a bamboo pole with me, which was used to mark the trail," Kuntz said. "I had it out in front of me, figuring I could use it to ward off any polar bears."

The whiteout lifted after 45 minutes. "I was fortunate," Kuntz said. "They have been known to last for days."

When you've gone to one pole, the desire to make a trip to the other is strong. Kuntz made it to the South Pole late in 1986. "I was on WEWS-TV's Morning Exchange show when Fred Griffith told me about his South Pole trip," Kuntz said. "The trip was sponsored by the National Science Foundation (NSF) in Washington, D.C." Kuntz wasted no time in writing letters to the NSF. In August 1986, he was notified that he was one of four media members chosen to make the trip.

Initially, UPI said it would fund the trip, but then backed out. "I looked at this as a trip of a lifetime," Kuntz said. "Even if I had to fund the trip on my own, I was going to do it."

The trip to the South Pole included stops in Los

In 1959, Kuntz befriends an Eskimo youngster on Greenland's ice cap.

Angeles; Honolulu; Christchurch, New Zealand; and McMurdo station, a research center south of New Zealand. It's the largest community in Antarctica - about 1,200 residents.

"We spent several days there and visited various scientific stations," Kuntz remembered. "One of the most spectacular places we saw was the ice caves near McMurdo Sound. The ice had a beautiful blue hue."

While near the open waters of McMurdo Sound, Kuntz also saw four Adele and two Emperor penguins. "None of them had any fear of man," he said. "We walked right up to them."

The trip to the South Pole was completed when Kuntz and the party he traveled with arrived at the Amundsen-Scott Base, a U.S. research station, in November 1986. The station is the southernmost continually inhabited place on Earth. "Our original flight there was aborted when we lost the No. 1 engine on our C-130 cargo plane," Kuntz said. "Secretary of the Navy John Lehman accompanied us on the second flight. I figured nothing was going to happen on that one."

The temperature upon arrival was a brisk -41°. The wind-chill was -75°. "There was not much to get photograph-wise," Kuntz said. "There was a lot of ice and snow, with just a pipe sticking out marking the exact location of the South Pole. Most photos were taken at the ceremonial South Pole."

The ceremonial South Pole is set up for pictures.

Kuntz at the South Pole ceremonial sign (top left), a pipe casting a shadow in the foreground marks the precise location of the South Pole (bottom left), and the entrance of the U.S. Amundsen-Scott Base at the South Pole (bottom right).

There is a red and white striped barber-like pole, capped with a metallic chromium globe, marking the spot. It is surrounded by 12 flags, representing the 12 Antarctic Treaty signees.

Several hundred yards away sits the geographic South Pole, which is marked by a small stake and a sign.

Kuntz has traveled the world in more than 50 years, with Paris, France, and Red Square in Moscow as two of his most memorable stops. "Someday," he said, "I'd like to get to Scotland and the Scandinavian countries."

Ice formations near McMurdo Sound.

Two emperor penguins at McMurdo Sound in Antarctica.

Tending a dog team at New Zealand's Scott Base in Antarctica.

Showing a camera to Eskimos at Baffin Island.

An Eskimo fisherman in Frobisher Bay.

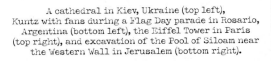

A cathedral in Kiev, Ukraine (top left),
Kuntz with fans during a Flag Day parade in Rosario,
Argentina (bottom left), the Eiffel Tower in Paris
(top right), and excavation of the Pool of Siloam near
the Western Wall in Jerusalem (bottom right).

The Dome of the Rock in Jerusalem (top right), the Congo River in Zaire (middle left), Kuntz tries his hand with the pan flute in Peru (middle right), and overlooking Cape Town, South Africa, harbor (bottom).

CHAPTER 10:
Prison Ministry

Texas inmate Kevin Hamilton reads a Bible in his cell.

Photographer Ron Kuntz has visited more than 2,000 prisons worldwide since the early 1970s as part of the Bill Glass Ministries. "Of all the things I've done," he said, "my heart is most moved by the prison ministries."

Over the years Kuntz befriended 13 death row prisoners who were eventually executed. "You would not be human if you did not get somewhat emotionally involved," Kuntz said. One death row prisoner Kuntz shot pictures of was Erica Sheppard, a Houston woman who was 21 years old when she helped murder a woman in a car-jacking. She confessed to the murder and was unrepentant at the time of her trial. "I saw her several different times," Kuntz said, "and took many pictures of her.

"After one visit, she sent me a letter. She asked me to send her some pictures, because she was going to be executed and wanted to see the pictures before she died. I thought this was rather unusual. She seemed more concerned with the pictures than her own execution."

Ironically, Sheppard was granted a stay of execution. She remains on death row, where she's been since June 1997.

The relationship Kuntz developed with Karla Faye Tucker, a convicted murderess, superseded any other. Kuntz first met Tucker in 1986 at the Mountain View Unit's death row in Gatesville, Texas. Tucker, an accomplice to two murders committed with a pickaxe on June 11, 1983, was tried and

Kuntz became friends with Karla Faye Tucker, the first woman to be executed in the U.S. since the Civil War.

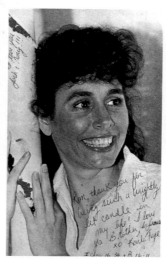

sentenced to death in 1984.

"During her trial," Kuntz said, "you would have wanted yourself to be part of throwing the switch to get rid of her. But, something happened to her as she awaited sentencing at the Harris County jail in Houston.

"A puppet show presented the gospel to the women and, as a result, Karla came to know our Lord." Kuntz communicated with Tucker on a regular basis following their first meeting. In November 1997, he received a letter saying she had a February 3, 1998, date for her execution. The months leading to her execution drew world-wide attention.

Kuntz was granted a two-hour visit with

Tucker in December 1997. "When I left the unit," Kuntz said, "I felt I would never see her again. I visited the Holy Land in January 1998, and when I returned home, there was a letter from Karla thanking me for the visit we had in December and for the pictures I made.

"It was a powerful, moving letter about how she was really looking forward to the execution. Even now, I have trouble reading the letter."

The day of the execution - February 3, 1998 - drew more than 200 media members from around the world to the Walls Unit in Huntsville, Texas. On that day, the governor's office received 12,519 calls running 4-to-1 against executing her. Nonetheless, at 6:20 p.m.

Pictured with four women (left to right) – Betty Lou Beets, Karla Faye Tucker, Frances Newton, and Pam Perillo – on death row at the Mountain View Unit in Gatesville, Texas. All except Perillo were executed.

Governor George W. Bush rejected a final plea for a 30-day stay of execution.

Tucker, whose last meal was a banana, peach, and garden salad with ranch dressing, was put to death by lethal injection 10 minutes later. "I certainly had a hard time when the execution took place," Kuntz said. "I thought if I was God, I certainly would have allowed her to remain on earth and have her testimony to the world. I was upset with God for not allowing her to get a reprieve.

"And, while I miss her very much, I realize now her going home was meant to be.

Bush came under fire for not commuting Tucker's sentence. Kuntz later received a letter from him. In it, he wrote, "According to the Texas constitution, the governor may commute a sentence only if the Texas Board of Pardons and Paroles recommends it. If the Board does not recommend commutation, the governor may grant only a one-time, 30-day stay of execution." Something which Bush chose not to do.

Some other prisoners Kuntz befriended through the years of accompanying Glass on his ministries included David Silva, Durham Stokes, and Kevin Hamilton.

In 1986, Silva was a 13-year-old incarcerated at the O.H. Close Youth Correctional Facility in Stockton, California. "He was locked up for stealing a car," Kuntz said. "He was a kid who had never known his father. I remember reading

DATE	NAME	TDCJ #	
2/3/98	KARLA FAYE TUCKER	777	EXECUTED (WHITE/FEMALE)
2/9/98	STEVEN RENFRO	999229	EXECUTED
3/11/98	JERRY HOGUE	660	
3/12/98	NORMAN GREEN	805	
3/24/98	LESLEY L GOSCH	842	
4/7/98	CARUTHERS ALEXANDER	704	
4/20/98	ERICA SHEPPARD	999144	(BLACK/FEMALE)
4/22/98	TIMOTHY GRIBBLE	929	
4/28/98	DESMOND JESSINGS	999161	
4/29/98	FRANK McFARLAND	963	
5/5/98	JAMES WILKINS	897	
5/7/98	BILLY HUGHES	556	
5/13/98	JOHNNY PENRY	654	
5/19/98	STACEY LOWTON	999066	
5/26/98	NAPOLINO BEAZLEY	999141	
6/8/98	WILLIAM DAVIS	614	
6/15/98	JAVIER S.MEDINA	944	
6/16/98	CLAUDE JONES	,980	

The holding cell where Tucker was placed prior to her execution at the Walls Unit in Huntsville, Texas (top left), Tucker waves goodbye following Kuntz's visit at the Mountain View Unit (top right), and the grisly leaflet showing those executed, and those scheduled to be executed, at the Ellis One Unit in Huntsville, Texas (bottom right).

a study many years ago stating that about 80 percent of the men and women incarcerated have no father image in their lives, meaning they didn't know their father or, if they had one, it was not a good relationship. So, his was not an unusual situation."

On this Sunday morning in 1986, Kuntz and yo-yo champion Bunny Martin were taking part in a chapel program, when a commotion took place. "One of the officers said a young person had tried to escape," Kuntz said. "I felt I had to speak to this person." Kuntz and Martin were granted permission to talk to the youngster following the program. "As the door of the cell opened," Kuntz said, "I saw this young man

crying. He covered his face with a blanket on the bunk bed."

Eventually, Martin brought out his New Testament and told Silva about the plan of salvation described in it. A tear welled up in the youngster's eye.

"David then prayed to receive Christ as Lord and Savior," Kuntz said.

Six years later, Kuntz attended a prison ministry seminar in Chicago. "David had spoken about his religious experience on a prison ministry video," Kuntz said. "He told what happened to him six years previously. What a blessing that was to me to find out that he was coming along."

Durham Stokes was a death row prisoner in

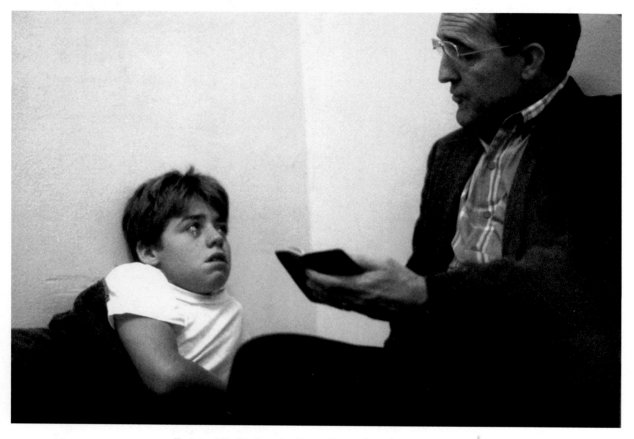

Kuntz met Yo-Yo champion Bunny Martin (right), who was with
David Silva (left) at the O. H. Close Unit in Stockton, California.

Florida, someone Kuntz never met, but felt he knew well. "I got a letter from him many years ago," Kuntz said. "He said that I didn't know him, but he was on death row at the Florida State Prison in Starke, Florida.

"He said he came to know the Lord while on death row and eventually his sentence was commuted to life." While serving time at the Florida State Prison, Stokes became friends with inmate David Wells. "David is someone who I had the privilege of leading to the Lord in the early 1970s," Kuntz said. "That's how Durham got in touch with me."

Stokes, who became an accomplished artist while in prison, sent Kuntz a Scripture-based painting about the two men walking to Emmaus when they had an encounter with the Lord. "It was my favorite passage of Scripture," Kuntz said. "I wrote to him saying he had done a fantastic thing that I would remember forever.

"Durham wrote back, saying that all his life he had hurt people and now he had done something positive even if it was while serving time in prison."

Kuntz and Stokes exchanged Christmas cards for years. But, one year, Kuntz's card was returned. On the envelope was written: deceased. "I never knew him," Kuntz said, "but one day when I've reached heaven, I am going to look him up."

Ron and Nancy Kuntz's fifth child, Josh, is a Down Syndrome child. Josh was born while Kuntz

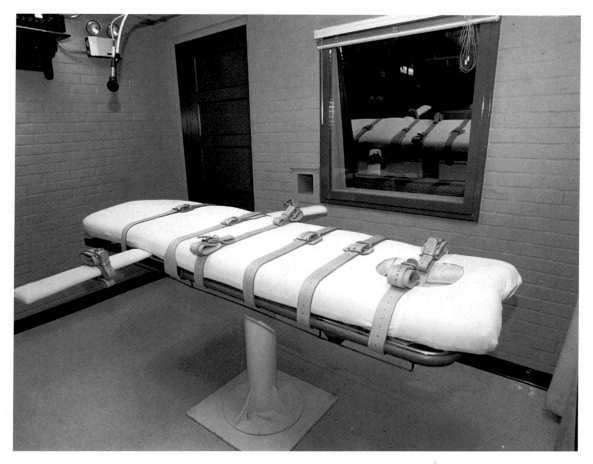

The gurney where the lethal injections take place at the
Walls Unit in Huntsville, Texas.

was covering the 1980 Moscow Olympics. "Josh was six weeks old when I returned home," Kuntz said. "I had not previously been told that he was a Down Syndrome child, but I sensed something was wrong when I first saw him."

Kuntz initially was upset at hearing the news. "I was bitter towards God for allowing this to happen. Our pastor told me that God gives special children to special parents. I told him that I didn't feel that special; why didn't God give that child to someone else."

A prison weekend in Melville, New Jersey, changed Kuntz's attitude. At the conclusion of a talk, Bill Glass asked the group if there was something they never thanked God for. Kuntz

stood up and thanked God for Josh. "From then on, I was able to share my story about Josh with many inmates over the years."

A few hours later, Kuntz was having dinner with several inmates. I asked one of the inmates, Nick, how he enjoyed the program, He said he really enjoyed it, especially when Bill Glass mentioned his grandson, who is a Down Syndrome child. Nick said he also had a Down Syndrome child."

Kuntz pulled out a picture of Josh. "I told Nick this was no accident that we met," he said. "I asked him if he ever trusted in Jesus as Lord and Savior and he said no.

"I asked him if he would like to at this very

A painting done by Durham Stokes while on death row at the Florida State Prison which he sent to Kuntz (left), a Christmas card from Kuntz to Durham that was returned marked "deceased" (below).

moment, and he said yes. Because of Josh coming into my life, an inmate had come to know the Lord."

One of the inmates with whom Kuntz shared his story about Josh was Kevin Hamilton, who was serving time in Texas. "Kevin found out Josh loved clowns," Kuntz said. "He painted one for Josh, which Josh hung in his room." In a letter, Hamilton mentioned that he was suffering from level-four throat cancer.

Several months later, at a prison weekend in Huntsville, Texas, Kuntz spent 45 minutes with Hamilton. "His tongue was swollen, and I had trouble understanding him," Kuntz said. Hamilton, knowing he was close to death, wrote down for his mother the hymn he wanted played at his

funeral. It was: 'Oh, for a thousand tongues to sing.' Hamilton died several months later.

Kuntz estimates he has participated in more than 300 prison weekends. "It means I have spent about 900 days in jail," he said. "Someone once suggested I have a free crime coming to me."

When he discovered that Kuntz's son Josh loved clowns, Texas inmate Kevin Hamilton responded by painting some clown scenes for him.

During his years in the prison ministry, Kuntz beheld many
provocative images, such as the electric chair at Florida State
Prison in Starke, Florida.

Bikers from the Christian Motorcycle Association, invited by Bill Glass,
roll down the death row corridor at the Ellis One Unit in Huntsville, Texas.

Inmates at the maximum security prison in Jackson, Georgia,
wile away the time with a game of chess.

Sign in San Quentin, north of San Francisco, makes it clear
to prisoners that guards shoot to kill.

Kuntz captured a member of the prison ministry team praying with
a death row inmate at the Holman Unit in Alabama.

Even in prison women prisoners can still give a friendly wave at the camera.

A Georgia inmate works on a puzzle in his cell

"Spiderman," (right) an inmate who got to know Kuntz, at
Soledad Prison Salinas, California.

Inmates communicate with each other and find out what is
going on in their wing using mirrors.